Gloucestershire
WORTHIES

PEOPLE AND PLACES

Saw this advertised in
"Evergreen".

Aylwin Sampson

with drawings by the author

WESTCOUNTRY
BOOKS

First published in Great Britain in 1996 by Westcountry Books

British Library Cataloguing in Publication Data
A CIP Catalogue Record for this book is available from the British Library

ISBN 1 898386 24 2

WESTCOUNTRY BOOKS
Halsgrove House
Lower Moor Way
Tiverton
Devon EX16 6SS
Tel: 01884 243242
Fax: 01884 243325

Printed and bound in Great Britain by Longdunn Press Ltd., Bristol

Introduction

Let us now praise famous men ... such as did bear rule ...
renowned for their power, giving counsel by their understand-
ing ... leaders wise and eloquent ... such as found out musical
tunes and recited verses in writing ... rich men furnished with
ability, living peaceably in their habitations ... All these were
honoured in their generations and were the glory of their
times.

I T IS WITH SUCH majestic words that the writer of Ecclesiasticus presents a
description of the great and the good. Those categories, kings, musi-
cians, poets and country gentlemen are as appropriate today as they
were all those centuries ago. Of course there are further 'sorts and
conditions' represent-ative of the intervening years: scientists, politicians
and sportsmen come readily to mind. Indeed many have been the attempts
to choose actual persons to typify what came to be called 'Worthies'.

In 1592 Richard Johnson made his selection of *The Nine Worthies of London*
and decided they should be chiefly military men, as indeed did Shakespeare in his Pageant of the Nine Worthies in *Love's Labour's Lost* though in
the text he names but five: Pompey, Alexander, Hercules, Judas Maccabaeus
and Hector. This limitation of nine seems to have been popular in an age
when the symbolism of numbers was potent. Sometimes the division was
into three groups of three: from the Bible, from the Classics, and from
Romance. Dryden puts it thus, 'Nine worthies were they called, of
different rites Three Jews, three pagans, and three Christian knights'.

It is however in architectural form that this celebration of the illustrious past
will be remembered by anybody who has visited the magnificent grounds
at Stowe in Buckinghamshire. For there is the Temple of British Worthies,

3

The Temple of British Worthies at Stowe.

designed by William Kent in 1732 for Lord Cobham. Such a display evoked a poetic description from his nephew Gilbert West:

> ... A sacred band
> Of Princes, Patriots, Bards and Sages stand;
> Men, who by Merit purchas'd lasting Praise,
> Worthy each British Poet's noblest Lays:
> Or bold in Arms for Liberty they stood,
> And greatly perish'd for their Country's Good:
> Or nobly warm'd with more than mortal Fire,
> Equal'd to Rome and Greece the British Lyre:
> Or Human Life by useful Arts refin'd,
> Acknowledg'd Benefactors of Mankind.

Who then are these Worthies which merited such a eulogy? Well, most could be expected after a cursory consideration of British history: Shakespeare, Inigo Jones, Pope, Bacon and Milton represent the Arts; Newton alone for the Sciences; Locke for philosophy; then for men of action and politics Drake, Raleigh, Hampden, the Black Prince; some predictable rulers, Elizabeth I, Alfred and William III; finally two odd choices, Thomas Gresham who founded the Royal Exchange, and strangest of all, John Barnard who seems to have gained a nîche because he 'distinguished himself in Parliament by an active and firm opposition to the pernicious and iniquitous practice of stock-jobbing'!

Maybe Barnard was a Worthy, but perhaps really he symbolises that other kind of person who featured in the tribute paid by Ecclesiasticus: 'And some there be ... who are perished as though they have never been ...' Or as the poet Gray puts it in his Elegy:

> Some village Hampden, that with dauntless breast
> The little tyrant of his fields withstood;
> Some mute inglorious Milton here may rest,
> Some Cromwell guiltless of his country's blood.
>
> Far from the madding crowd's ignoble strife,
> Their sober wishes never learned to stray;
> Along the cool sequestered vale of life
> They kept the noiseless tenor of their way.

Thomas Fuller in his compilation, *The Worthies of England* published, after his death, in 1662, presents a selection quite as mixed as any other's, but interestingly there is a decision on his part to treat them geographically: 'Why the worthies in this work are digested county-ways ... it is as inform-ative to our judgements to order them according to their place as by centuries according to the time; seeing "where" is as essential as "when" to a man's being ... Here you may behold how each county is innated with a particular genius inclining some in one profession, some in another; one carrying away the credit for soldiers, another for seamen, another for lawyers, another for divines ... Here also one may see how the same county was not always equally fruitful in the production of worthy persons, but, as trees, have their bearing and barren years ... Nor let a smaller shire be disheartened to contest with another larger and more populous, seeing *viri* do not always hold out in proportion to *homines*.' For Gloucestershire, Fuller has assembled 24 'notables'; eight of them churchmen of varying memorableness – who has firm recollection of John Sprint, priest, who died in 1623 or John Carpenter, bishop of Worcester, died 1476? – county landowners, a barrister, a mayor, martyr, and a vice-admiral. There is but one woman.

Which leads naturally to two questions: were all of Fuller's Worthies natives of the counties covered, and would today's collection have the same condition or indeed the same distribution of vocations?

The answer to both must be, No, and anyway there has been since his day much more fluid movement from county to county, even, it must be said, of the boundaries of the counties themselves. And as for the sorts of Worthies, perhaps the following might be a modern version of Ecclesiasticus: The Arts: that is including architecture, music, the stage and writing; The Sciences: medicine and exploration, invention and discovery; Society: the church, philanthropy and reformation, war, commerce, sport, ... aristocracy and, indeed, eccentricity!

It is surprisingly easy to fit most of the Worthies into one of these compartments, and equally easy to link them to a place, whether by birth, death or something else between. For this latter reason and also because Fuller argued the case well, the entries in this collection are by place rather than person. It is perhaps only when one attempts such a gazetteer that the richness and diversity of Gloucestershire's Worthies become apparent. Doubt-less some names will be unfamiliar, others may be found in unexpected places, and indeed a few may not appear at all, either because they belong to somewhere which is no longer within the county's borders, or maybe space did not permit their inclusion. It is also possible that the compiler has inadvertently omitted them. If so, what better demonstration could there be of –

> *Absentes tamen laudem suam habent;*
> *Nec obscuriores obliviscuntur*

> (The absent have their own praise;
> Nor are the obscure forgotten)

Ablington

J. Arthur Gibbs

It was to the Elizabethan manor house that **J. Arthur Gibbs** came after enduring two years in a London office. Here he wrote *A Cotswold Village* which, by its publication in 1898, led legions of books on the character and beauty of the area. Sadly he was granted only a few years of living there, for at the age of thirty-one he died.

Adlestrop

Since 1553 the Leigh family had been closely associated both as landowners of the Park and also as rectors. One, the **Rev. Thomas Leigh** was an occupant of the rectory when Jane Austen, a niece, visited in the last years of the eighteenth century.

The Old Rectory, Adlestrop.

7

But it was **Edward Thomas** who popularised the place by his poem of the same name, over a hundred years later.

Alderley

There are two important houses in this village on the edge of the Cotswolds. The seventeenth century Mount was the last home of **Marianne North**. Born in 1830, she devoted herself to flower painting, and when forty years old, after her father's death, travelled to all parts of the world in search of subjects. Her fine collection was acquired by Kew, where a gallery perpetuates her memory. Her memorial can be seen in the churchyard, and there was a sundial at the Mount to the memory of her opossum mouse. She died in 1890.

Another naturalist lived at the nearby Grange. **Brian Hodgson** from the age of eighteen worked for the East India Company and for twenty three years travelled in Nepal. On his return to England in 1858 with a collection of 10,500 birds he wrote authoritatively on the zoology of that area, and became through his knowledge of Tibet an exponent of Buddhism. He lived to be ninety-five.

The Grange was also the birthplace of **Sir Matthew Hale**. He lived from 1609 to 1676, and had a distinguished career in law. After Oxford and Lincoln's Inn, he held the posts of Justice of the Common Pleas, Chief-Baron of the Exchequer, and finally Chief Justice of the King's Bench. In 1713 he wrote a *History of the Common Law*, following it with a *History of the Pleas of the Crown* in 1636. A man of his time, his well-balanced views were tempered by a belief, however, in the occult and in witchcraft.

Matthew Hale

Amberley

Rose Cottage was Dinah Mulock's home whilst she write much of her novel *John Halifax, Gentleman*. It was published in 1857, by which time she had married the nephew of a partner in the publishing firm Macmillan, so she is better known as **Mrs Craik**.

Another house in this hillside village, St Loes, was the setting for the painting, by **Charles Gere**, *Plucking the red and white roses in the Temple Gardens* which depicted the start of the War of the Roses, and was widely reproduced in schools after its display in 1908.

Mrs Craik

The poet **Sydney Dobell** came here in 1853, and **P.C. Wren** the author of *Beau Geste* is buried in the churchyard.

Ashleworth

Rose Cottage, Amberley.

Ferrying rights across the River Severn here have been held by the **Jelf** family, of the Boat Inn, since 1643, when Charles I fleeing from Gloucester after its siege bestowed the privilege to the landlord for his service in rowing him over.

The Boat Inn, Ashleworth.

9

Manor Farm, Aston-sub-Edge.

Aston-sub-Edge

Patron of the arts, servant to James I, Groom of the Bedchamber to Charles I, **Endymion Porter** entertained Prince Rupert at the Manor Farm. Something of a poet himself, it was his friend Robert Herrick, who praised him in the lines:

> Let there be patrons, patrons like to thee,
> Brave Porter, poets ne'er will wanting be.

Endymion Porter

Exiled in Holland, he died in 1649, and is buried in London's St Martin's-in-the-Fields.

Dover's Hill was the site of the 'Olympicks' organised by **Captain Robert Dover** in 1612, dressed in a suit of royal clothes given by the King. These games survived as an annual event till 1852, when rowdy crowds made them undesirable.

Burnt Norton's original manor house of 1620 has survived the fate of its adjacent successor which was set fire to by **Sir William Keyte**, MP for Warwick, in 1741. He perished in the flames; by accident or design is uncertain. Its name and gardens feature in **T.S. Eliot's** *Four Quartets*, of 1943.

Awre

This could be called the birthplace of church singing, for in 1562 **John Hopkins**, who lived here, and Thomas Sternhold from nearby Blakeney, brought out their *Whole Booke of Psalmes*. These metrical versions provided for almost two hundred years the hymnody of parish churches.

Berkeley

Edward Jenner

Born in 1749 the son of the vicar, **Edward Jenner** was apprenticed to a Chipping Sodbury surgeon. In 1770 he went to study under the great John Hunter at St George's Hospital, London, returning to Berkeley three years later. There he set up as a country doctor, acquiring a large practice. He was elected to the Royal Society for a paper on the cuckoo, but his claim to fame rests of course on his discovery in 1796 of vaccination as a protection against smallpox. His home where he died in 1823 is now a museum, and its garden still has the rustic hut where he gave vaccination to the poor free of charge, as indeed he did when, from 1795 to 1815, he lived in Cheltenham.

Alpha House, Cheltenham where Edward Jenner of Berkeley give free vaccinations.

The castle, occupied by the **Berkeley** family since the fourteenth century, was the scene of Edward II's murder in 1327.

In 1888 **John Fitzhardinge Butler** was born, to distinguish himself as the first Gloucestershire soldier to win the Victoria Cross in the First World War.

Berry Hill

This village on the edge of the Forest of Dean was the birthplace in 1935 of **Dennis Potter** the playwright who made television his medium. Of his many productions *Brimstone and Treacle, Pennies from Heaven, The Singing Detective* and *Lipstick on your Collar* are best remembered. A final poignant interview only weeks before his death from cancer was shown on television in 1994.

Dennis Potter

Bisley

From 1827 to 1873 **Thomas Keble**, and then until 1902 his son, also Thomas, were vicars here. The former provided the elaborate wells, and the family possibly created the legend of the Bisley Boy. This story supposed that a local boy became the substitute for the child princess Elizabeth when she suddenly died at Over Court, by the church, and had to act out his life as Queen, when the time came.

John Keble was married here.

The large parish includes a number of hamlets. One is Upper Lypiatt where Lypiatt Park, dating from the fourteenth century, has associations through **John Throckmorton** with the Gunpowder Plot, as letters from his relative Winter, Catesby and Tresham raising suspicion led to its discovery.

Here from 1957 lived **Lynn Chadwick**, the sculptor.

At Nether Lypiatt the manor house was built at the end of the seventeenth century for **Charles Coxe**, a judge and chief justice for the counties of Brecon, Glamorgan and Radnor, MP for Cirencester and Gloucester, and Clerk of the Patent Office. But such public duties have been eclipsed by a legend that he promised a reprieve to a blacksmith in return for making elaborate gates to the house, and on their completion had the man hanged nonetheless. It is said that the gates swing open inexplicably each anniversary, 25 January, and indeed that the place is haunted.

However such tales did not deter **Princes and Princess Michael of Kent** from buying it in 1980, nor Mrs **Violet Woodhouse** in 1923. She was a noted keyboard musician and broadcaster, as well as hostess to such visitors as Osbert Sitwell and Harold Nicolson.

Blakeney

Co-author of many collections of metrical psalms **Thomas Sternhold** was also Groom of the Robes to Henry VIII and Edward VI. He was born here in 1500.

Blockley

Formerly a prosperous town with many silk mills, and the first to be lit by electricity, it had strong associations with the prophetess **Joanna Southcott**. She was born in Devon in 1750; by 1802 she was in London 'sealing the faithful'. From 1804 to 1814 Rock Cottage in Blockley was her refuge, and at her death she left the celebrated box which she asserted would cure the world's problems if opened in the presence of 24 bishops of the Church of England.

The town has close association also with Northwick Park where the **Spencer-Churchills** received visits from their cousin Winston, and the **Warner** family who owned much of New York and Philadelphia. **James Rushout** bought Northwick Park, becoming a member

Rock Cottage, Blockley.

Northwick Park, Blockley.

of Parliament in 1660 when only seventeen. Created baronet the following year, he served as MP for thirty years, and died in 1698 before being able to take up appointment as an Ambassador Extraordinary.

Bourton-on-the-Water

The character actor **Wilfred Hyde-White**, memorable for his parts in the films *The Third Man*, *My Fair Lady*, and *The Browning Version*, was born at the rectory. He died in 1991, aged 87.

Dudley Graham Johnson, born here in 1884, was awarded the Victoria Cross only seven days before the end of the First World War.

Wilfred Hyde-White

Brockhampton

Adjacent to Sevenhampton, this hamlet, though not possessing its own church, has a large mansion and a colourful character to go with it. In 1788 George III came to lunch here, but it is **Fulwar Craven** who made

Brockhampton Park his home, and it was he who drove around in a yellow gig, wore flowered waistcoats and a white beaver hat. He it was whose passion was horse-racing, indeed he nearly won the 1839 Derby, and whose practical jokes made him the talk of the Cheltenham area.

Grandson of the Hon. Charles Craven, Governor of Carolina, Fulwar asserted his connection with the Berkeley family, and alleged Brockhampton Park had been his father's home too. Perhaps his most astonishing claim was that George III invited him to call during the Royal residence in Cheltenham. However, a simple calculation reveals that Fulwar would have been only three years old in 1788.

Maybe eccentrics can be allowed such extravagancies.

Brockworth

The antiquary **John Theyer**, born at nearby Cooper's Hill, died in 1673 and was buried in the churchyard here. His grandfather, another John Theyer, married the sister of **Richard Hart**, the last prior of Lanthony, a man also concerned for historical records, because at the Dissolution of the monastery he rescued the valuable manuscripts, which in the course of time became part of the King's Library in the British Museum. Hart was responsible too for the fine half-timbered east wing of Brockworth Court.

Bussage

Despite the claims of Ilchester in Somerset, there are grounds for assigning Toadsmoor here as the birthplace in 1214 of **Roger Bacon**, the Francisan monk who envisaged aeroplanes, telescopes and magnifying glasses. Such dabbling in science, magic or alchemy resulted in his imprisonment and the charge of heresy.

Charlton Kings

Though now incorporated into Cheltenham, the identity of this place has been preserved, not least by its former residents.

Coxhorne, Charlton Kings, a home of Sydney Dobell.

Sydney Dobell, best known for his poems *The Roman* and *Balder*, lived here from 1840, first at Coxhorne and later at Detmore, used by **Mrs Craik** in her *John Halifax, Gentleman*. Another house, Hetton Lawn, was built by the Rev. George Liddell whose grandchild Alice together with **Lewis Carroll** instigated in 1863 the idea of *Alice through the Looking Glass* there.

Charlton Kings' Hetton Lawn where Alice Liddell's grandparents lived.

For seven years in the 1930s, **Cecil Day-Lewis** lived at Box Cottage, and to pay for roof repairs wrote the first of his detective stories as 'Nicholas Blake'. He became Poet Laureate in 1968, and professor of poetry at Oxford.

Thomas Robins was born here in 1715, a painter mainly in water-colour, whose speciality was the depicting of country houses in their setting. Through the discovery of one such picture the original layout of Painswick House and its rococo garden was revealed.

Box Cottage, Charlton Kings, home of C. Day-Lewis.

Another artist, **Briton Riviere**, though not a native came to live in Charlton Kings when his father William, also a painter, decided his son should attend Cheltenham College. Animals were Briton's particular strength, his most popular work being the painting of child with collie dog entitled *Sympathy*. He married a member of the Dobell family, and died in 1920.

Clara Burton came from an illustrious family. Her father was a general, eight of her nine brothers were in the Services, and she achieved some distinction as an artist. Portraits in pastels, as well as oils were exhibited at Birmingham, Liverpool and Manchester Galleries. She died in 1947.

Other notable inhabitants who served with distinction include Admiral **Sir Charles Wager** who was born here in 1666, becoming commander-in-chief at Jamaica, a privy councillor and First Lord of the Admiralty. He died in 1744 and is buried in Westminster Abbey. His father incidentally was captain of a ship in the fleet bringing Charles II back to Britain at his restoration.

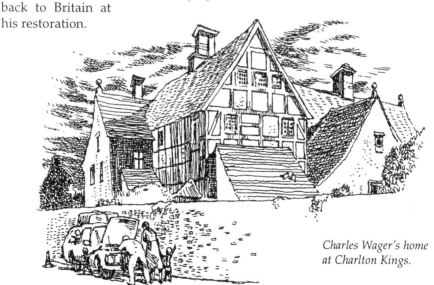

Charles Wager's home at Charlton Kings.

Cheltenham

The emergence of this spa town in the late eighteenth century attracted fashionable society for relatively short stays. But there were many people of importance who were born here or made their permanent residence in its Regency environment.

Gustav Holst

The arts are well represented. Foremost must be **Gustav Holst** who was born here in 1874. Educated at the Grammar School and the Royal College of Music, he is particularly remembered for his composition *The Planets*. Another composer, who came to the town in 1841, was **John Barnett**. Sometimes called 'the father of English Opera', he had his *Mountain Sylph* parodied in Gilbert and Sullivan's *Iolanthe*. Nevertheless he was notable as a singing teacher here. For forty-five years the violinist **Marie Hall** lived here till her death in 1956. In 1921 she gave the first performance of Vaughan Williams' *Lark Ascending*.

The theatre's debt to Cheltenham includes **Ralph Richardson** who was born here in 1902, as was the leading dramatic actress of her time **Lillah McCarthy** in 1875, though in her case she gave up her stage appearances twenty-five years before her death in 1960. Another great Shakespearean actor **Charles Macready** came to the town in 1860 at the age of sixty-seven,

Ralph Richardson

J. Elroy Flecker

Gustav Holst's birthplace in Cheltenham.

ostensibly to retire, though he busied himself lecturing and giving dramatic readings – like Charles Dickens who in fact visited him here.

Literary people associated with the spa town are represented by **Alfred Lord Tennyson** who lived here from 1843 to 1850. Part of his *In Memoriam* dates from this period. The son of Dean Close School's first headmaster was **James Elroy Flecker**. His *Hassan* dates from his years as a vice-consul in Beirut, but the poem *November Eves* is set firmly in Cheltenham. He died in 1915, and lies in Leckhampton churchyard. **Thomas Haynes Bayly** died in the town in 1839. A somewhat tragic figure, his sentimental ballads were mercilessly parodied, though *The Mistletoe Bough* has weathered better. A more robust poet was **Adam Lindsay Gordon** whose boyhood was spent here. His passionate love of horses found inspiration in race meetings both in Cheltenham and later in Australia. He committed suicide in 1870, and is the only Australian poet commemorated in Westminster Abbey. Finally in the literary field, **A.C. Bradley**, born 1851 in the town and educated at

The home of Thomas Haynes Bayly in Cheltenham's High Street.

John Forbes' house in Montpellier Villas.

Cheltenham College, became a formidable commentator and critic, being Oxford's professor of poetry from 1901 to 1906.

In the visual arts, **Robert Smirke**, the architect of the British Museum, lived for the last sixteen years of his life here, and was buried in 1867 in Leckhampton churchyard. Other notable architects, who contributed to Cheltenham's nineteenth century townscape were **Samuel Daukes**, the **Jearrads**, **John Middleton**, **John Forbes** and **J.B. Papworth**. On a lighter note, England's foremost entertainer in the world of Victorian magic was born and worked in Cheltenham. Descendant of an Astronomer Royal, **John Nevil Maskelyne** was a watchmaker who turned to producing illusions and automata in London's Egyptian and

Montpellier Street workplace of John Maskelyne.

St George's Halls. He also invented a typewriter, a ticket punch, a coin-operated lock, and filmed Queen Victoria's Diamond Jubilee!

For the sciences in their broadest sense Cheltenham can claim a variety of eminences. The aircraft designer **Frederick Handley Page** was born here in 1885 and educated at the Grammar School. **George Dowty** on the other hand came here in his early twenties and stayed to build the engineering firm that bore his name. Somerset-born **Benjamin Baker** was only four when his family moved to Cheltenham. He went to the Grammar School and from there to an illustrious career in engineering too, culminating in the Forth railway bridge of 1883.

Edward Wilson born here in 1872 is honoured as one who died with Captain Scott in the Antarctic Expedition of 1911. But he should also be remembered as a doctor, botanist and artist. Another explorer and artist was **Charles Sturt**. After his pioneer expeditions to Australia he came to live out his retirement in Cheltenham, dying here in 1869. The founder of the Medical Missionary Society, **Dr Thomas Colledge** spent many years in

Edward Wilson

Francis Close

Charles Sturt

Dorothea Beale

Richard Pate

China before returning to Cheltenham, whereas the work of **Josephine Butler** in campaigning for the repeal of the unjust Contagious Diseases Act began in 1864 when her family moved to Liverpool from the town.

Of the churchmen who came here, the most memorable was the **Rev. Francis Close**. His years, as incumbent of the parish church, 1824 to 1856, earned him the reputation of being a fine preacher, and an implacable opponent of horse-racing, the theatre and railways. His support for education, though, resulted in many schools and colleges from infant to teacher training being founded here. One of them, Cheltenham Ladies' College, owed much of its development to **Dorothea Beale** who 'ruled' from 1858 to 1906 as its second Principal.

From an earlier age, the contribution of **Richard Pate** to education was the Grammar School he founded in 1586. Born at Cheltenham in 1516, and educated at Corpus Christi, Oxford, he proceeded to Lincoln's Inn. Significantly he became a commissioner for confiscating the property of chantries, in 1546, and Recorder for Gloucester ten years later. An MP for the city twice, he died in 1588 the year of the Spanish Armada.

The town's military reputation grew from the large number of retired Indian army officers and officials who favoured the place. One such was Lt General **Sir Charles Napier**. A cousin of Charles James Fox, he was a short-sighted sickly child, but his military career showed him a brave soldier. In October 1848 he came to Cheltenham, but his retirement was curtailed the following year by his being recalled to command a further campaign in India. On successful completion of the Scinde Campaign he is reputed to have sent home the terse despatch 'Peccavi' (I have sinned). Incidentally his statue is one of only four in London's Trafalgar Square.

A more recent war leader **Arthur Travers Harris**, was born in Cheltenham in 1892. He became known during the Second World War as 'Bomber Harris', for from 1942 till the end of hostilities he organised RAF Bomber Command's offensive against many cities in Europe.

Arthur Harris

But, sporting 'heroes' must have a place too. The cricketer **Gilbert Jessop** was born here in 1874. Succeeding W.G. Grace as captain of the county eleven in 1900, he scored 26,058 runs including 53 centuries in a career which ended in 1914, though he did not die till 1955. **Fred Archer** too was Cheltenham born, but his life tragically ended early with suicide brought about by his need to keep his weight down, and the necessity of much travelling to race-courses. Nevertheless his reputation as a leading jockey for seventeen years was unchallenged. In 1886 that record of 2148 winners was finalised by his death.

Fred Archer

One other suicide must be added, that of **Duncan Gordon Boyes**. He was born in Cheltenham in 1846, and as a midshipman on *HMS Euryalus* won the Victoria Cross in 1864. But after being so honoured, he broke rules about entering a naval yard, was dismissed the service, and at the age of twenty-three ended his own life. Other Victoria Cross winners who were born in the town include **Arthur Forbes Kilby**, awarded in 1915, **William Fraser McDonell**, awarded in 1857 during the Indian Mutiny, **Richard Annesley West** who lost his life 1918, and **James Forbes-Robertson**, awarded in 1918.

Paragon Terrace, home of Duncan Boyes.

Cheltenham has had its colourful, even eccentric, figures as well as heroes. **Miles Watkins** reputedly discovered, at the age of seven, a hoard of guineas, and was himself discovered by a Duchess of Devonshire at nine. She took to his intelligent face and even more to his telling her the local tale of Maude's Elm. His subsequent career, patronised by her, was erratic. From being a shoemaker he progressed to the position of private secretary to James Webb, a philanthropist who gave away much of his annual income of £75,000. Watkins died in 1844, having acquired the sobriquet 'King of the Cheltenham Royal Family'.

Chipping Campden

It was to this honey-coloured stone town that **C.R. Ashbee** brought his East End workers of the Guild of Handicraft in 1902, inspired by the Arts and Crafts movement. This large-scale project involved over 100 men and was based at the old silk mill in Sheep Street. A year later **F.L. Griggs** the fine topographical artist joined them. He lived at Dover House in the High Street, appropriately named, for he persuaded the National Trust to buy Dover's Hill, site of the Olympick Games started by **Robert Dover** in 1612. Griggs provided the illustrations for many of the *Highways and Byways* books published early this century; his volume on Oxford and the Cotswolds, 1905, was largely responsible for his moving to the town.

Ernest 'Chinese' Wilson, born here in 1876, was notable as a plant hunter and after his years travelling in China became curator of the

The old silk mill, Chipping Campden.

F.L. Griggs' home, Dover House, at Chipping Campden.

Massachusetts Arboretum. He is commemorated in his home town by a memorial garden just next to the old rectory garden where it is said the use of willow bark as aspirin was first introduced.

The actor **Sir C. Aubrey Smith** though born in London, in 1863, spent his boyhood here when his father became the town's doctor, having as his home the Cotswold House Hotel. He attended the local Grammar School before going to Cambridge where he gained a cricket 'blue' for four successive years. In fact his prowess at the game earned him a place in the Sussex eleven, and the captaincy of an England tour to Australia in 1887. But it is his film career which is most remembered, with leading parts usually as an irascible soldier in *The Four Feathers, Lives of a Bengal Lancer, The Prisoner of Zenda, Little Lord Fauntleroy* and *The House of Rothschild*. He died in 1948.

The Ernest Wilson Memorial Garden, Chipping Campden.

Perhaps the most dramatic, even bizarre, character associated with the town was **William Harrison**. Steward for fifty years to Lady Juliana Noel, daughter of Sir Baptist Hicks, Harrison aged seventy disappeared for two years in 1660. Suspicion fell on the Perry family who were hanged for his assumed murder. On Harrison's return unharmed, the absurd story he told of abduction and escape has perplexed historians ever since. Not surprisingly, the episode has come to be known as 'The Campden Wonder'. John Masefield wrote a play in 1907 about it, and books and articles have grappled with the enigma.

Graham Greene

From 1931 to '33 **Graham Greene** rented 'Little Orchard', a thatched cottage up a Mud Lane. There he worked on

The Friends Meeting House at Broad Campden, associated with Jonathan Hulls.

his novels *Rumours at Nightfall* and *Stamboul Train* as well as a biography of the 2nd Earl of Rochester. Another writer **H.J. Massingham** lived in the town, and was inspired to produce in 1932 his book *Wold Without End*, centred on the area.

In nearby Broad Campden the unfortunate **Jonathan Hulls**, a clock repairer, conceived the idea of a ship propelled by steam power. But his experimental craft, tried out on the river at Evesham, was ridiculed as a failure. However, his portrait did earn an honoured place on the stateroom wall of RMS *Queen Mary*, and his other invention, the slide-rule, has not proved useless. He died in 1758.

Churcham

One of its sons, **Alfred Henry Hook**, won the Victoria Cross at Rorke's Drift in 1879 during the Zulu War.

Cinderford

The popular broadcaster **Jimmy Young** was born here. He made his first broadcast in 1949, in 1955 was the first British singer to have consecutive 'hit' records, and began his 'Jimmy Young Show' in 1973.

The poet **Leonard Clark** grew up in this Forest of Dean town, drawing much of his inspiration from the area. Though born in the Channel Isles in 1905 his formative years were spent here, and before moving to London he taught for eight years in Gloucestershire.

Cirencester

Lord Bathurst's and his friend **Alexander Pope**'s names are paramount in the story of this town's development: the former because of his building of Cirencester House with its monumental yew hedge; the latter because of his involvement with the landscaping of the extensive park. Begun in 1718, their activity attracted such visitors as Lord Burlington, John Gay and Swift.

Pope's 'seat' in Cirencester Park.

Chesterton House was the home of 'Rajah' **Sir Charles Brooke** who restored order to Sarawak, while **Joseph Howse's** exploration of Canada, merited a pass to be named after him. But perhaps Cirencester should be most proud of another explorer **Sir William Edward Parry** who commanded five Arctic expeditions, the last in 1827 penetrating further than any previous one.

Joseph Knipe lived in Chester Street whilst teaching at the Upper School, though he is remembered as the founder of Wolsey Hall, Oxford, a correspondence college whose students have included Nelson Mandela.

In the medical field there was Sir William Parry's father **Caleb Hillier Parry**. Born in 1755 his early years were spent in Gloucester Street, and he went to the local grammar school where he struck up a lasting friendship with Edward Jenner. After qualifying as a physician he practised in Bath, but his work included identifying the cause of angina and thyrotoxicosis, as well as the mechanism for the pulse. Elected a FRS, he died in 1822, a year after Sir William was similarly honoured.

Clearwell

This Forest of Dean village has a Gothic Revival castle of 1727 where the Wyndham family lived; **Caroline, Countess of Dunraven**, relative of the Irish politician Earl, inherited in 1810, and stayed till her death sixty years later. Another occupant was Col. Charles Vereker, cousin of Lord Gort VC.

But the VC most remembered here is that awarded to Private **Francis Miles** who won it in October 1918, and lived till 1961.

Cleeve Hill

Emblem Cottage, Cleeve Hill.

The highest part of the Cotswolds, its scarp has splendid views of the Malverns. On its slope is Emblem Cottage, hon.e of **George Stevens**, the jockey who rode in 15 Grand Nationals, won five, and who died in 1871, falling from his horse in neighbouring Southam village.

Another resident on Cleeve Hill was the Polish-born science writer and broadcaster **Jacob Bronowski**. He lived here whilst Director of the Coal Board's Fuel Research Centre at Stoke Orchard. He is chiefly remembered for his study of William Blake, and the television series called *The Ascent of Man*.

Bronowski's house on Cleeve Hill.

Coberley

Only a doorway from the churchyard remains to indicate the site of the Berkeley family's Hall. As the widow of Sir Thomas married Sir William Whittington of Pauntley Court in the west of the county, it is possible that **Richard Whittington** the younger son grew up, or even was born, here.

Coleford

At Newland Street **Mary Howitt** was born in 1799. Author of children's stories with her husband William, she is remembered chiefly for the poem '"Will you walk into my parlour"? said the Spider to the Fly'. Her parents had come here from Staffordshire when David Mushett an ironmaster had been developing steel production methods. It was Bessemer, incidentally, who patented the process in 1856 and **Robert Mushett**, David's son, who was born in Coleford, derived little benefit from his patent of the same year. However he had greater success with his 'R. Mushett Special' steel which generated a future array of tool tungsten alloys.

Angus Buchanan was twenty-two when he won the Victoria Cross in Mesopotamia in 1916.

Coln St Aldwyns

John Keble was curate here during the last ten years of his father's fifty-three year incumbency. The manor house in 1896 was the home of **Sir**

Michael Hicks-Beach, Chancellor of the Exchequer, whose earlier relative of the same name had restored Williamstrip Park nearby, a property originally owned by **Henry Powle**, Speaker of the House of Commons, in the early seventeenth century.

Cowley

Inseparate from the malted milk he formulated, **Sir James Horlick** lived in the Manor from 1895. Though born in Ruardean, Forest of Dean, his interest in this village can be judged from the estate houses and school bearing his name. A substantial table tomb in the adjoining churchyard marks his death in 1921.

James Horlick's grave at Cowley.

Cranham

From January 1948 to September 1949 **George Orwell** stayed as a patient at the Cotswold Sanatorium amongst the extensive beech woods here, in a vain attempt to arrest his tuberculosis. The poet **James Elroy Flecker** also came thirty-eight years earlier after his diagnosis as a consumptive had been established at Constantinople, where he was vice-consul.

There are associations too with the composer Gustav Holst. His tune to 'In the bleak mid winter' is Cranham, a reminder of his mother's stay here.

George Orwell

31

Prinknash Abbey, Cranham.

Prinknash Abbey nearby had many visits from the artist **W. Heath Robinson** before the First World War, as his son, Alan, had entered the Order.

Warren Hastings' memorial in Daylesford churchyard.

Daylesford

The churchyard brings together three names that have been household words in their day: **Warren Hastings** who rebuilt the family house despite his impeachment trial after being Governor General of India; **Esmond Cecil**

Warren Hastings

Harmsworth, 2nd Viscount Rothermere who owned Daylesford House, long after Hastings died in 1818, and was chairman of the *Daily Mail*; finally, the son of a Daylesford rector, **F. H. Grisewood** who died in 1972 having been chairman of the BBC *Any Questions?* programme for many years.

Didbrook's rectory where Peter Warlock lived.

Didbrook

Philip Heseltine, better known as the composer **'Peter Warlock'** lived at the vicarage here in 1913, studying with the Rev. Hubert Bancroft-Allen. The intention was to gain a high enough standard in classics for entry to Oxford University, though after a year he left – not to join up on the outbreak of war, for he had been pronounced medically unfit – but perhaps because of his temperament. However, he did make frequent returns to Didbrook, a girlfriend being the attraction. And he also rented at Crickley Hill a cottage, where his unpredictable behaviour included riding a motorcycle at night stark naked! Such erratic traits and swings of mood plagued him till his early death at thirty-six in a gas filled Chelsea room. The *Capriol Suite*, and other orchestral works, songs and carols are his musical legacies.

Down Ampney

The tune to the hymn 'Come down, O Love Divine' bears the name of this village, having been composed by **Ralph Vaughan Williams**. Born at the vicarage in 1872, he spent only two and a half years here because on his father's death the family had to move.

Ralph Vaughan Williams

33

Down Hatherley

The Gwinnett family produced men who contributed to the development of Cheltenham, but one, **Button Gwinnet**, is remembered further afield. He became Governor of Georgia and signatory to the Declaration of Independence. Unfortunately he also became victim to a duel, dying in 1777.

Duntisbourne Rouse

Pinbury Park was the last home of **Sir Robert Atkyns** who lived here till 1711. His country history *The Ancient and Present State of Gloucestershire* was published the year after his death. The son of an MP, Chief Baron of the Exchequer and Speaker of the House of Lords, he was himself MP for Cirencester and a barrister.

The Ledbury-born poet and novelist **John Masefield** lived here from 1933 till the outbreak of the Second World War, as did the architect and furniture craftsman **Ernest Gimson** and the **Barnsley brothers** at the end of the nineteenth century. Indeed the son of Sidney Barnsley, Edward, was born here in 1900 becoming also a noted furniture designer.

Pinbury Park, Duntisbourne Rouse.

Dursley

Born about 1496 **Edward Fox** was by 1528 involved with Cranmer in the matter of Henry VIII's marriage to Catherine of Aragon. Its annulment saw his advancement. In 1532 he was granted goods and chattels of all suicides in England, and three years later this Dursley boy was bishop of Hereford.

Another success story was that of **Robert Ashton Lister**, born 1845. He set up his agricultural machinery manufacturing firm here after a rift with his father's woollen machinery business. However, by the following century his son Percy had developed the production of light diesel engines and it is for these that the firm is chiefly known.

Ashton Lister

Lister's chief engineer in the 1890s was **Mikael Pedersen** who invented the 'safety bicycle' which the firm manufactured. He also invented the milk churn. But despite these successes he died in poverty in 1929 back in his native Denmark, though in 1995 his remains were re-buried in Dursley.

Dymock

In 1637 at the White House opposite the church, **John Kyrle** was born, whose education followed at Ross-on-Wye and Oxford, and who in the subsequent years lived at Ross, building churches and hospitals. Pope praised him, and in 1877 the Kyrle Society formed for improving the lot of the poor. 'The Man of Ross' died in 1724.

John Kyrle's birthplace, Dymock.

Little Iddens

May Hill

Dymock Church

Ryton Firs

The Old Nail Shop

Glyn Iddens

If Dymock lost a philanthropist, it gained many poets. In 1911 **Lascelles Abercrombie** came to live at Ryton, then **Wilfred Gibson** followed in 1913 to 'The Old Nailshop', and the next year saw the American **Robert Frost**, **Edward Thomas** and **Eleanor Farjeon** join this brief flowering of a literary settlement. Here came also **Rupert Brooke** and **John Drinkwater** as visitors to add their lustre to the writing.

Edge

The 'incomparable **Max**' Beerbohm lived here briefly in 1947, and at Stockend hamlet **C. Henry Warren** who wrote *A Cotswold Year* published in 1936.

Elmore

There had been since the thirteenth century land here belonging to the Guise family. It was **Christopher Guise** who, by his loan to the exiled Charles II, secured a baronetcy. Later personalties included **Sir Berkeley William Guise**, warden of the Forest of Dean, Lt-Col in the Gloucestershire Militia, MP for Gloucester from 1811 till his death in 1834, and **Sir John Wright Guise**, commander of the Scots Guards in the Napoleonic Wars, honoured for bravery by Queen Victoria, and Senior General in the Army.

Berkley William Guise

Perhaps however the most intriguing member of the family was **William Guise**. He accompanied Edward Gibbon to Italy in 1764 when the mighty *History of the Decline and Fall of the Roman Empire* was conceived. Gibbon also saved William from fighting a duel by persuading him to apologise to the challenger. At his death in 1783 William left £1000 to Gloucester Infirmary.

Fairford

Churchman, writer and driving force behind the Oxford Movement, **John Keble** was born in the family home here in 1792. It was not until 1835 that he left the town permanently to become rector of Hursley in Hampshire. His popular collection of readings, *The Christian Year,* came out in 1827.

John Keble

The American artist **Edwin Austin Abbey** came to England in 1878 aged twenty-six, and lived here for some years.

John Keble's birthplace at Fairford.

The stained glass in the parish church is a lasting memorial to the Tame family. **John Tame** was a wool merchant, and, together with his son, Sir Edmund, who received Henry VIII here, and grandson, another Edward, who was invited to join the retinue at the Field of the Cloth of Gold, they made, in the words of Leland, 'Fairford to flourish'.

Flaxley

The only monastery in the Forest of Dean, Flaxley Abbey, 1148, owed its founding to the mysterious hunting accident which befell Milo, Earl of

Flaxley Abbey.

Hereford, on Christmas Eve 1143, an event similar to that which killed William Rufus in the New Forest. It was owned by **Sir William Kingston** after the Dissolution. He, as Constable of the Tower of London, superintended Anne Boleyn's beheading in 1536. His son, Sir Antony, was in charge when Bishop Hooper was burnt at the stake at Gloucester nineteen years later.

Mrs Catharine Boevey, whose dissolute husband died in 1692, lived here until her death in 1772. She was a great benefactor of the Three Choirs Festival as well as a founder of the Society for Promoting Christian Knowledge, but Addison immortalised her as the 'perverse widow' courted by Sir Roger de Coverley in *The Tatler*.

Catharine Boevey

Forthampton

Born in Tewkesbury 1905, the boyhood of **Henry Yorke** was spent at the family home in nearby Forthampton Court. After Eton and Oxford he joined his father's engineering firm in Birmingham, and during the Second World War served in the Auxiliary Fire Service. To the literary world though he was known as 'Henry Green', the idiosyncratic even eccentric writer who produced such novels as *Blindness*, *Loving* and *Living*, before his output abruptly ceased in his forties.

Henry Yorke

38

Frampton-on-Severn

The Clifford family have associations here, and the persistent tradition that **Jane Clifford**, 'the Fair Rosamond' of Henry II, lived at the Manor Farmhouse is strengthened by its location on the north side of Rosamond's Green.

Gloucester

Of Roman origin, possessing a masterpiece of medieval architecture, co-founder of the oldest music festival in the world, this city whose name the county takes has a rich and diverse number of Worthies to offer.

The evangelist **George Whitefield**, born in 1714 at the Bell Inn, Southgate Street, was educated at both the King's School and the Crypt School in the city before going to Oxford. There he joined the Wesleys' Methodist Club, and became ordained in 1736. His preaching began back in Gloucester and extended to

George Whitefield

39

Georgia two years later. Debarred from pulpits in England because of his Nonconformist associations, he concentrated on both open-air preaching, and trans-Atlantic congregations, making seven visits to America, helping in educational projects like the founding of schools and colleges including Princeton, before dying in 1777 at Newburyport, Massachusetts.

Although not born in this county, **John Hooper** is indelibly associated with its diocese, for as the second bishop, he was a victim of Queen Mary's persecution being burned at the stake just outside his cathedral precinct in 1555.

John Hooper

A native of the city, **Robert Raikes** was born in 1736. Educated, like Whitefield, at the King's and Crypt schools, his apprenticeship to his father's *Gloucester Journal* led to his taking over in 1757 the family business. However it was his concern for the aimless young people on Sundays which earned him national recognition. Setting up Sunday Schools to provide worthwhile activity proved so successful that the idea spread rapidly to other cities. He died at his home, Ladybellegate House in Longsmith Street, Gloucester, in 1811.

Raikes' house, Gloucester.

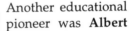

Robert Raikes

Another educational pioneer was **Albert Mansbridge** born in the city in 1876. He instigated a scheme in 1903 which developed into the Workers' Educational Association, he himself becoming its General Secretary.

As befits its membership of the Three Choirs Festival, Gloucester's contribution to music has been considerable. **Ivor Gurney** began his tragic life in 1890 at Queen Street, and at the age of ten was a chorister in the cathedral. Friendships with Herbet Howells and Fred W. Harvey developed his own leanings to composition both in music and poetry. But service in the trenches

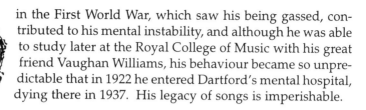

Ivor Gurney

in the First World War, which saw his being gassed, contributed to his mental instability, and although he was able to study later at the Royal College of Music with his great friend Vaughan Williams, his behaviour became so unpredictable that in 1922 he entered Dartford's mental hospital, dying there in 1937. His legacy of songs is imperishable.

Another chorister, but from an earlier time, **John Stafford Smith** was born in the cathedral close in 1750. He became a Gentleman of the Chapel Royal and indeed played the organ at a Three Choirs meeting, but his chief claim to distinction rests on his composing the tune of *The Star Spangled Banner*, adopted officially by the United States Congress in 1931. His death in 1836 was somewhat ignobly caused by a grape pip lodged in his throat.

John Stafford Smith

The musician who contributed immeasurably to raising the standard of singing in cathedrals held the position of organist of Gloucester for the last eleven years of his life. **Samuel Sebastian Wesley** had occupied similar posts at Hereford, Exeter and Winchester, but he found each a struggle, though out of them came a rich harvest of anthems, hymn tunes and chants still used today by choirs. He died at Gloucester in 1876 aged sixty-six. Born in this city, **Herbert Sumsion**, on the other hand, lived to be ninety-six, and his legacy of settings for services was matched by a tenure at the cathedral organ which lasted from 1928 to 1967. Pitched into a Three Choirs Festival by the sudden death of his predecessor Sir Herbert Brewer, the twenty-nine year old Sumsion made such a success of the challenge that Elgar produced his memorable observation, 'What at the beginning of the week was assumption has now became a certainty'.

Samuel Sebastian Wesley

W.E. Henley

Three natives of the city must be included as representative of other arts: **Philip Wilson Steer**, 1860-1942, became a notable artist particularly in watercolour; **Charles Gere** born in 1869 was chiefly a tempera painter; and **W. E. Henley**, 1849-1903, who, apart from being the original of Long John Silver in his friend Stevenson's *Treasure Island*, promoted the work of Kipling and H.G. Wells, James Whistler and Auguste Rodin. As a poet, his best remembered lines are:

I am the master of my fate:
I am the captain of my soul.

In the sciences, there is **Charles Wheatstone**. Born in Westgate Street in 1802 and apprenticed to his uncle, a musical instrument maker in London, Charles invented the concertina, the stereoscope and with W. F. Cooke the first public telephone. But his name is perpetuated in his Wheatstone Bridge, a device for measuring electrical resistance.

Charles Wheatstone

Gloucester has had its eccentrics, too. Perhaps the most celebrated was **James** or 'Jemmie' **Wood** who inherited the drapery and banking business founded by his grandfather in 1716. His astute dealings combined with a miserly disposition resulted in his leaving on his death in 1836, at the age of seventy-nine, an estate worth £900,000. **John Taylor**, born here in 1580, was a strange mix of professional waterman, who once travelled the Thames estuary in a brown paper boat towed by fish, and a poet who produced verse lampoons. He became subsequently a Yeoman of the Guard, and was buried at his death in 1653 at St Martin's-in-the Fields.

John Taylor

Hardwicke

In 1726 the **Yorke** family bought this estate near Gloucester, and both father Philip, and son Charles achieved eminence as lawyers. Each became Lord Chancellor, and Charles's son in due course was a Home Secretary. Honours were also heaped on the family, culminating in an earldom.

The Court, which **Barwick Baker** inherited in 1841, became eleven years later his reformatory school. Here he began with eight delinquent boys, but by the time the establishment closed in 1922 over 1600 young offenders had been educated.

Highnam

In 1838, the twenty-two year old **Thomas Gambier Parry** bought Highnam Court. His inherited wealth and cultured disposition, enriched by a Grand

Tour which he undertook after Cambridge, fitted him for a life at Highnam engaged not only in work on the house but also in mural art elsewhere. He developed techniques in ecclesiastical decoration at the cathedrals, notably Ely and Gloucester. The death of his first wife instigated the building of Highnam's 1851 church, with its interior embellishment his own responsibility.

Thomas Gambier Parry

His son **Hubert Parry** succeeded to the estate in 1888 at the age of forty. Remembered as a composer of such works as *Blest Pair of Sirens* and the tune to Blake's *Jerusalem*, he was Director of the Royal College of Music, and Professor of Music at Oxford. He died in 1918.

Highnam Court.

During the Indian Mutiny, **John Christopher Guise** who was born at Highnam in 1826, won the Victoria Cross.

Hubert Parry

Kempsford church.

Kempsford

In turn army officer, coal merchant and inmate of a debtors prison, **George Hanger** was one of the great eccentrics. He refused to use his title as the 4th Lord Coleraine, wrote on such topics as the lives of eminent gamesters, horse and dog care, the defence of London against invasion, even predicting in 1801 the American Civil War sixty years early. His abiding fear was that the Devil would claim him, so he ordered his coffin should be above ground in the church here. Unfortunately when an organ was installed it had to be placed over him, thus creating an even more bizarre arrangement!

In 1803 he auctioned his house of Driffield, enabling purchasers to take away parts they had bought. He died in 1824 and his character was delicately put on the family memorial at Driffield, as 'He was a practical Christian as far as his frail nature did allow him to be so.'

Kilcot

At Beavans Hill House, on a former cider farm, **Rutland Boughton** lived from 1927 till his death in 1960. Here he composed his last four music dramas, two symphonies and other minor works. He is chiefly remembered for his *The Immortal Hour*.

Rutland Boughton

Beavans Hill House, Kilcot.

Kingscote

Edward Jenner, the discoverer of vaccination, married Catherine Kingscote here in 1788. Her family had lived at the Grange since the twelfth century, as their many monuments in the church testify.

King's Stanley

Anthony Keck, the architect of many country houses in Gloucestershire, died here in 1797. And **Percival Scrope Marling** was born here in 1861. He distinguished himself in the King's Royal Rifle Corps by winning the Victoria Cross in the Sudan in 1884.

Lechlade

Anthony Keck's home, King's Stanley.

Percy Bysshe Shelley is remembered here for his *Stanzas in a Summer Evening Churchyard* which were composed after a visit in 1815. He and his companions Mary Godwin, Thomas Love Peacock and Charles Clairmont had rowed from Windsor.

Lechlade.

Leonard Stanley

In July 1939 the artist **Stanley Spencer** came to the White Hart Inn, paying £1.10s a week for his room. George and Daphne Charlton accompanied him during the two years he was here, and she features in his painting of the Wool Shop, modelled on one in Regent Street, Stonehouse. A scrap-book of drawings entitled *Us in Gloucestershire* is another reminder of this period in his life.

Lydney

The composer **Herbert Howells** was born at 41 High Street in 1892. After studying at the Royal College of Music he concentrated on church music, his *Hymnus Paradisi* being a good example of his work that earned performances at the Three Choirs Festivals. His ashes were interred in Westminster Abbey, but the family memorial is at Twigworth churchyard.

Herbert Howells

Howells' birthplace at Lydney.

Matson

Built by **Richard Pate** about 1575, Matson House had its most notable occupants in 1643 when King **Charles I** made it his headquarters during his siege of Gloucester. He had his two sons, the future Charles II and James II, with him and in fact they stayed here for a longer time.

Minchinhampton

In 1768 at Box House two physicians, **Browne** and **Hayward** reputedly carried out smallpox vaccination, that is some thirty years before Jenner's paper on his own experiments.

James Bradley, the Sherborne astronomer who died in 1762, is buried here.

One mile south east stands Gatcombe Park, built in 1771 for the Sheppard family and in 1814 sold to the stockbroker **David Ricardo** whose *Principles of Political Economy and Taxation* was published three years later. He died here in 1823. Bought in 1937 by **Samuel Courtauld**, the house passed to his son-in-law **R. A. Butler** ten years after. But pressures of public life prevented his living much here, and in 1976 it was purchased by the Queen as a home for her daughter **Princess Anne** and Mark Phillips.

David Ricardo

Minsterworth

Although Hartpury was his place of birth in 1888, Redlands Farm here became the childhood home from the age of two for **F. W. Harvey**. After schooldays at the King's School Gloucester where he struck up a friendship with Ivor Gurney, and at Rossall, he qualified as a solicitor. However in 1914 he enlisted in the county regiment, distinguishing himself in action in France. From this war experience as soldier and prisoner some of his finest poetry emerged. But a return to Gloucestershire saw him deteriorate and his death in 1957 was a sad end to a promising poet.

Miserden

The former rectory, now Sudgrave House, became in 1948 the home of **Pat Smythe**. From 1947 to 1964 she represented Britain in the Olympic show-jumping team, and her commitment to horses had further expression in such autobiographical writing as *Jump for Joy* and *Leaping Life's Fences*. Her early riding experience took place at the home of her uncle, Swindon Manor, near Cheltenham. She died in 1996.

Pat Smythe

Moreton-in-Marsh

A King's Bench judge for fourteen years and chairman of the Coal Commission which advocated in 1919 that the mines be nationalised, **John Sankey** was Lord Chancellor from 1929 to 1935. He died in 1948, eighty-two years after his birth in this town.

Nailsworth

Born at Newport, Monmouthshire in 1871, and living in the USA for a number of years where he lost a leg 'jumping' a train, **W. H. Davies** spent the last nine years of his life here at various houses. 'Glendower' was the final one, where incidentally a neighbour who spitefully blocked Davies' outlook across the valley dropped dead soon after! Best remembered by the *Autobiography of a Super Tramp* published in 1908:

> What is this life, if full of care,
> We have no time to stand and stare?

two novels and much poetry, including those lines, came from his pen.

At 'The Lawns', Spring Hill lived **George Archer-Shee** who was expelled as a cadet from the Royal Naval College Osborne in 1908 for allegedly stealing a postal order. Defended by

W.H. Davies

W.H. Davies' final home at Nailsworth.

Sir Edward Carson he was acquitted. The episode provided the basis of Terence Rattigan's play *The Winslow Boy*.

Newnham-on-Severn

In the Church, rebuilt in 1881, there is the funeral hatchment of the widow of Sir Humphry Davy, inventor of the miner's safety lamp, and in the Severnside streets of this town can be seen evidence of the products from the first factory in England to use coal as fuel for glass-making. That was in 1620, and in fact the first greenhouse was made here for Sir Edward Mansell.

Newnham House is reputed to be the original house in the novel *East Lynne* by **Mrs Henry Wood**. She also founded the *The Argosy* magazine in 1867.

Just upriver, Broadoak is the real-life setting for John Masefield's play *The Tragedy of Nan*, whose name part was first created by Cheltenham-born Lillah McCarthy.

Newnham House, Newnham-on-Severn.

King's Mill, Painswick.

Oakridge

Bradford-born **William Rothenstein** bought Iles Farm in 1912, making it home from his London duties as director of the Royal College of Art, till 1922. He then moved into a nearby cottage.

Winstone's Cottage on the farm was where **Max Beerbohm**, that urbane writer and caricaturist, spent the years of the First World War. He never came to terms with country living, always being immaculately dressed as for London, even to the spats. No sooner had he moved out than **John Drinkwater** took up residence from 1918 to 1921.

Painswick

To this hillside town **Charles I** came in 1643, during the Civil War, establishing himself briefly at the Court House; indeed a royal proclamation survives with the words 'at our court at Painswick'.

Another Charles came here and stayed somewhat longer. **Charles Gere** was born in 1869 trained at the Birmingham School of Art, becoming a tempera painter. He identified himself with the Arts and Crafts movement, and produced many pictures inspired by the Cotswolds. His drawing of Kelmscott Manor appeared in William Morris's *News from Nowhere*. He settled in Painswick in 1904, till his death in 1957.

At King's Mill, one of the mills built in the valley, **Gerald Finzi** lived from 1922 to 1926; he composed his *Severn Rhapsody* and the cantata *Dies Natalis* here. He had spent part of his childhood nearby, at Chosen Hill, Churchdown.

Gerald Finzi

Pauntley

As the Whittington family had owned till 1545 the land near Upleadon on which the present sixteenth century Court stands, there is a probability that Sir William's younger son **Richard Whittington** was born here. His subsequent career culminating as Lord Mayor of London in 1397, 1406 and 1419 belongs as much to pantomime as history.

Pauntley Court featured in 1933 when the Poet Laureate **John Masefield** was actively involved in its conversion as a home for the unemployed and homeless. Of the £2000 needed, Masefield provided £750 from giving poetry readings. The scheme for these Wayfarers as they were called survived until the home closed in 1940.

Richard Whittington

Prescott

The early eighteenth century Prescott House near Gotherington was converted from farmhouse to Gothic hunting lodge when it was bought in 1848 by the Earl of Ellenborough who had been Governor General of India from 1841-1844 and then was living at Southam Delabere. It is said that he installed two Indian concubines here.

In 1920 the twelve-year old **Francis Bacon** lived here during his short time attending Dean Close School in Cheltenham; and in the late 1940s the BBC motoring correspondent, **B. H. Hartley**, was its occupant, appropriate for a house that stood at the end of a Bugatti Club speed hill climb.

Prestbury

Although Cheltenham-born, **Fred Archer** grew up here at the King's Arms public house where his father, a noted steeplechase jockey who had won the Grand National in 1858, was landlord. The brilliant but short career of Fred, ended with his suicide in 1886.

Randwick

Simon Pearce went out to Australia in the nineteenth century and developed part of Sydney which he named after this village.

But another person, **John Elliott**, chose to stay here, for he was vicar for seventy-two years.

Rendcomb

The celebrated Gloucestershire families of Tame and Guise most closely associated with Fairford and Elmore respectively have each possessed the estate here. However in 1863 **Sir Francis Goldsmid** bought it, demolished the mid-seventeenth century house, building the magnificent Italian style mansion and stables. He also laid out the grounds, planting copses which spelt out his name in Hebrew characters.

Perhaps most importantly **Samuel Rudder** wrote here his *New History of Gloucestershire* 1779.

Rodborough

In 1757, the manor estate was bought by a Woodchester clothier who bequeathed it, and his baronetcy, to his son in 1774. So began **Sir George Onesiphorus Paul's** great work as a prison reformer. For when he became, six years later, High Sheriff and Chairman of the Quarter sessions the full impact of conditions in the county's gaols made him resolve to devote his energies and influence to change things. By the time of his death in 1820, prisons had been built that gave healthier, purposeful and just treatment to the inmates.

George Onesiphorus Paul

Benjamin Bucknall was born in 1833 of a family that had already produced one architect. Benjamin's designs were epitomized by the uncompleted mansion at Woodchester, and his career by his move to Algiers where he was able to satisfy his grand schemes in houses for English, French and Arab patrons.

Rodmarton

The name **Lysons** is almost synonymous with Rodmarton. Beginning with the Rev. Samuel, and continuing with his two sons Samuel, a barrister, and

Daniel who succeeded his father as rector, there was a strong tradition of historical research. All three were Fellows of the Society of Antiquaries. Daniel, born in 1762, chaplain to Horace Walpole, wrote and illustrated *Magna Britannia*, and after inheriting the family estate, *A History of the Three Choirs Festival*. His brother Samuel, a year younger, was also an artist, exhibiting at the Royal Academy as well as publishing *Views and Antiquities in Gloucestershire* and *Roman Antiquities of Woodchester*.

Further generations of Lysons became clergymen, and men of military action: Sir Daniel was Constable of the Tower of London 1816-1898, and his son **Henry** who lived from 1858 to 1907 won the Victoria Cross.

St Briavels

It is difficult to associate this village with its impressive castle gateway with the great cricket grounds of this country and Australia. Yet here was born a man unique in that game. **William Evans Midwinter** emigrated to the

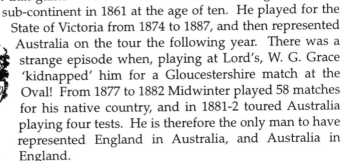 sub-continent in 1861 at the age of ten. He played for the State of Victoria from 1874 to 1887, and then represented Australia on the tour the following year. There was a strange episode when, playing at Lord's, W. G. Grace 'kidnapped' him for a Gloucestershire match at the Oval! From 1877 to 1882 Midwinter played 58 matches for his native country, and in 1881-2 toured Australia playing four tests. He is therefore the only man to have represented England in Australia, and Australia in England.

William Midwinter

Saintbury

Rector here till his death in 1545, the classical scholar **William Latimer** translated Aristotle, was a friend of Grocyn and Linacre, as well as being tutor to Cardinal Pole. Before coming to Saintbury he had been rector of Wotton-under-Edge.

Salperton

The founder of *Picture Post* and the children's magazine *Eagle*, **Sir Edward**

Hulton bought the estate here in 1951, with the intention of using the house for relaxation and entertaining his colleagues from the publishing world, as well as turning the rest into a model farming community. The concept lasted thirty years, and Hulton himself died shortly after in 1988.

Sapperton

Though his mansion is now only a field's bumps, **Sir Robert Atkyns** has his memorial in the church where his bewigged effigy is holding a representation of his masterwork *The Ancient and Present State of Gloucestershire* published the year after his death in 1711. His final home was at Pinbury Park in neighbouring Duntisbourne Rouse, and by a strange reversal it was from that house three leading craftsmen made the change to Sapperton three centuries later. **Ernest Gimson**, together with **Sydney** and **Ernest Barnsley** left Pinbury Park when Lord Bathurst revoked the lease; they took up his offer of sites to build or restore places here, and used Daneway House as the workshop for their funiture-making enterprise. When Gimson died in 1919 the workshop closed, though both the Barnsleys continued their architecture profession and, again strangely, both died in 1926.

Charles Mason born here in 1730 became assistant at Greenwich observatory to another Gloucestershire native, James Bradley of Sherborne. Asked

by Lord Baltimore and a Mr Penn to define the boundary between the 'slave and free' states in 1763, Mason with his collaborator the surveyor Jeremiah Dixon settled on what has since been known as the Mason-Dixon Line, dividing Maryland and Pennsylvania in the United States.

Sezincote

There could well be justification for stating that Brighton's Royal Pavilion owes its existence to **Sir Charles Cockerell**. For it was his Indian-style house here, designed by his brother, S. P. Cockerell, which so captivated the future

Robert Atkyns' tomb, Sapperton.

Prince Regent on his visit in 1807. That Calcutta ever came to the Cotswolds was because Sir Charles, and indeed his father, made fortunes from careers with the East India Company, though perhaps his uncle Samuel Pepys Cockerell, by his designs for Warren Hastings' Daylesford house, had provided additional inspiration.

Charles Cockerell

Sherborne

Born here in 1693 and educated at Northleach Grammar School and Balliol College Oxford, **James Bradley** became a clergyman at Bridstow and in Pembrokeshire. Even when he was made Savilian Professor of Astronomy at Oxford in 1721 he lived at Wanstead in Essex where his uncle was rector. However, after marrying a Susannah Peach of Chalford in 1744, two years after being appointed Astronomer Royal, Greenwich became his home, though he died in 1762 at Chalford and was buried at Minchinhampton. His great contribution to astronomy was establishing the positions of the fixed stars.

Slad

For many people this village and its surrounding countryside have become familiar as the setting of *Cider with Rosie*, the autobiography of the early years of *Laurie Lee*. He was born here in 1914, and at the age of nineteen walked to London, going from there on foot through Spain with its Civil War, returning over the Pyrenees. As well as writing two further volumes of autobiography, he prepared scripts for wartime documentary films, a verse play for radio, and composed poetry.

Laurie Lee

Slimbridge

Traditionally honoured as the birthplace of **William Tyndale** in 1495, it was from here that the first translator of the Bible into English went on to Cambridge University and then to Little Sodbury manor where he was chaplain and tutor to the Walsh family. But his most significant work as writer and translator was done on the Continent because of persecution. Tragically, it was at Vilvorde he met his death by strangulation in 1536.

Snowshill

It was whilst serving in the First World War that **Charles Wade** saw an advertisement for the manor house, and on his demobilisation bought the

derelict place. His training as an architect coupled with his family proper-
ties in the West Indies enabled him to restore the building and gardens;
while his collecting mania was indulged to such effect
that the house became a treasure trove of bicycles,
musical instruments, Japanese armour, toys, model farm
wagons, to name but a few of the contents of its
22 rooms. In 1951 Wade gave it all to the National Trust
and went back to St Kitts. However on a visit
to Snowshill in 1956 he fell ill and died in Evesham
hospital. He is buried in the churchyard here.

Charles Wade

Southrop

The Old Vicarage might be termed a home of the Oxford Movement for it
was here that in the 1830s **John Keble** had his university friends like
Froude, Williams and Wilberforce during the vacation to study sessions.

The Old Vicarage, Southrop.

Standish

Here, near Stonehouse, was a hunting lodge built in 1830 which Lord
Sherborne occupied whilst his grand house at Sherborne was being rebuilt.
Then it was let to **Richard Potter** who was influential in several ways, for in

addition to being a director of the Great Western Railway and the Hudsons Bay Company, he also had nine daughters, including Mary Playne, founder of the Gloucester Training College in 1892, and Beatrice who married Sidney Webb in that same year, thus comprising that formidable pair of social reformers. Another sister, Theresa, became the mother of Sir Stafford Cripps, Chancellor of the Exchequer in 1947, remembered chiefly for the policy of austerity he introduced.

Stanway

The great manor here was appropriated at the Dissolution of the Monasteries by the Tracy family, and its descendants included the **Earl and Countess of Wemyss**. They hosted house parties in the first half of the twentieth century which included such distinguished names as G. K. Chesterton, H. G. Wells, Walter de La Mare, and the cricket enthusiast J. M. Barrie, who even persuaded the Australian touring eleven of 1921 to play here, and who provided at his own expense the thatched pavilion.

The nearby hamlet of Wood Stanway produced **William Edgar Holmes** who gave his life in France a month before the Armistice of 1918, winning the Victoria Cross at the same time. He was twenty-three.

Stanway House gateway.

Cricket pavilion, Stanway.

Stinchcombe

The Georgian Piers Court was the first home that **Evelyn Waugh** had, it being a wedding present from Lady de Vesci, grandmother of his wife Laura. From 1937 to 1956 the Waughs lived here, Evelyn reluctantly being involved slightly in village matters: he was chairman of the Parish Council in 1946, and had been president of the Dursley Dramatic Society since 1938 without ever meeting a member in fifteen years! But it was here that his writing flourished, resulting in such works as *Brideshead Revisited* in 1945, *The Loved One* 1948, *Men at Arms* 1952, *Officers and Gentlemen* in 1955. Despite his many walks and twice weekly visits to Dursley cinema, the place eventually palled, and Waugh left 'Stinkers' for Combe Florey in Somerset.

Evelyn Waugh

Stancombe Park had greater attraction for the **Rev David Edwards**, vicar of nearby North Nibley from 1859 to 1881, for when he married its owner he made a garden that was not only a fantasy of romantic settings, but by its secretive location away from the house led to stories of his clandestine trysts with a gipsy girl.

Another clergyman, the Welsh poet and tractarian, **Isaac Williams** spent his last seventeen years here, dying in 1865.

Stancombe Park, Stinchcombe.

Stoke Orchard

The half-timbered cottage called Old Rowley was in 1938 the home for a famous flyer. **Amy Johnson** had just been divorced from Jim Mollison, her world-record solo flights to Australia and Cape Town were behind her, and she had been rejected by the Civil Air Guard even as a reserve pilot. Small wonder that her stay here passed largely unnoticed. Soon after, she joined the Air Transport Auxiliary, and in 1941 she lost her life over the Thames estuary.

Old Rowley Cottage, Stoke Orchard.

Amy Johnson

Stow-on-the-Wold

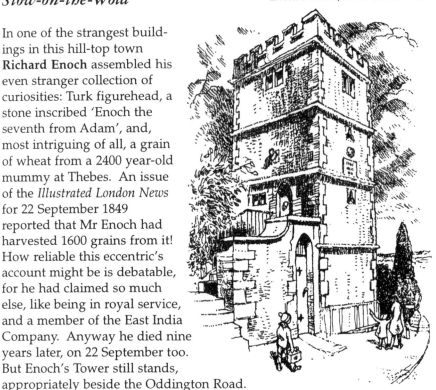

Enoch's Tower, Stow-on-the-Wold.

In one of the strangest buildings in this hill-top town **Richard Enoch** assembled his even stranger collection of curiosities: Turk figurehead, a stone inscribed 'Enoch the seventh from Adam', and, most intriguing of all, a grain of wheat from a 2400 year-old mummy at Thebes. An issue of the *Illustrated London News* for 22 September 1849 reported that Mr Enoch had harvested 1600 grains from it! How reliable this eccentric's account might be is debatable, for he had claimed so much else, like being in royal service, and a member of the East India Company. Anyway he died nine years later, on 22 September too. But Enoch's Tower still stands, appropriately beside the Oddington Road.

Stroud

Born here in 1718, **John Canton** became a schoolmaster in London. But he is remembered in the world of physics as the inventor of the electroscope and electrometer. His was the first powerful artificial magnet, and in 1762 he conclusively proved that water could be compressed.

In 1881 **Frederick Delius** stayed at 'Fort William' near Butterow, not to compose music but to gain experience with the Baxter family's knowledge of woollen cloth manufacture. For Bradford-born Delius came from a similar background.

Frederick Delius

To Stroud also came **Edmund Kean**, as an itinerant actor, and it was during his period performing at the Bedford Street theatre that he married Mary Chalmers, in the parish church. The churchyard, incidentally, has the grave of Lt. Delmont, who took part in England's last duel.

Another lieutenant, in the Worcestershire Regiment this time, Stroud-born **Eugene Paul Bennett** won his Victoria Cross in France in 1916 at the age of twenty-four.

Born in Hampshire where his parson father had a model railway in the garden, and later living at Box in Wiltshire near to the GWR line, the **Rev. Wilbert Awdry** turned almost instinctively to inventing stories about locomotives when his three year old son Christopher had measles. From these the extraordinarily popular children's books featuring Thomas the Tank Engine emerged. It must be added that Mr Awdry has written other works for adults on steam railways and industrial archaeology. For thirty years this place has been his retirement home after ministries in East Anglia.

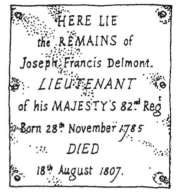

Grave of Lt. Delmont in Stroud Churchyard.

Temple Gutting

Sir Richard Deane was a Parliamentarian during the Civil War, rising to be a major general in Cromwell's New Model Army and an admiral in the Commonwealth Navy. Appointed a commissioner to try Charles I, he was a signatory to the subsequent death warrant. After his own death in 1653 at the naval engagement with the Dutch at Solebay, his body lay in State before burial in Westminster Abbey.

Tetbury

Originally Huguenots, the Paul family's prosperity enabled them to build Highgrove in 1796, a house which was subsequently to suffer fire and rebuilding. However it proved attractive enough for the son of a prime minister, **Maurice Macmillan** to buy it in 1965, and the son of a USA president, Elliott Roosevelt, to rent it for two years. And in 1980 it became fit for a future king when the **Prince of Wales** became its owner.

A cousin of the Paul family, **Sidney Austyn Paul Kitcat** was born in Tetbury in 1868. His career as a cricketer is memorable, not just because he played for Gloucestershire, sharing in a ninth wicket partnership with W. G. Grace when 193 runs were scored, but also that he was responsible for the MCC altering its law regarding bowlers not changing ends more than twice in an innings.

On her marriage, **Alice Liddell**, the major figure in Lewis Carroll's immortal books, left Cufnells in the New Forest and came to live at Upton House here.

Born in Tetbury in 1872, **Alfred Ernest Ind**, a shoeing smith with the Royal Horse Artillery won Gloucestershire's only Victoria Cross of the Boer War.

Tewkesbury

The 'Annerley' of **Mrs Craik's** *John Halifax, Gentleman* where Abel Fletcher's mill still stands, and the 'Elmbury' of John Moore's books which centre on this town, Tewkesbury can claim associations with a number of notable persons.

John Moore

At Gupshill Manor, Queen Margaret stayed before the decisive and bloody battle in May 1471; at the Tudor House the writer **John Moore** lived for most of the first eleven years of his life. His 35 books, together with his involvement as organiser of the pre-Second World War Tewkesbury Festival and post-war director of the Cheltenham Literature Festival, are remembered by his museum in Church Street. He died in 1967 aged 59.

Church Street too was where the Cartland family lived. Major Bertram was killed in 1918, his sons Ronald and Anthony killed at Dunkirk, but his daughter **Barbara Cartland**, born in 1901, became a writer of romantic novels which have almost created a genre of their own.

More serious reading would have been the lot of students at Academy House, later to be the Tudor House of John Moore. For in 1712 **Samuel Jones** a Presbyterian minister from Pennsylvania opened a Dissenters Academy for those men debarred from university by their religious affiliation. Strange therefore that of the students one became an archbishop of Canterbury, others bishops of Durham and Worcester, while one proceeded to the Lord Chancellorship of Ireland.

Stranger still was the **Rev. C. Grove** who, apart from donating the organ that perpetuates his name to the Abbey, had an inordinate fear of being eaten by worms. Accordingly he had a mausoleum built in 1897 with a 4 feet thick concrete floor, buttressed walls and heavyweight tiles, to withstand an earthquake, let alone earthworms. Inside lead coffins were installed, and as his wife died first, he used to go and read to it!

Thrupp

A worker at John Ferrabee's Phoenix Foundry in the 1820s was **Edward Beard Budding**. In 1830 having been inspired by equipment in the parent

Thrupp Cloth Mills, he patented not only the adjustable spanner but also 'a machine which country gentlemen may find in using an amusing, useful and healthy exercise'. It was the lawn-mower.

Toddington

A family which went back to Emma, wife of Ethelred the Undready, included the notorious **William Tracy**, one of the four murderers of Thomas Becket. Later members adopted the name Hanbury-Tracy, and one **Charles Hanbury-Tracy** designed the second manor house here in 1820. As member of parliament and chairman of the selection commission to choose designs for the new Houses of Parliament he generously withdrew his own submission in favour of Charles Barry's!

Uley

Born here in 1726, the son of a vegetarian pigkiller, **Samuel Rudder** set up as a bookseller and printer in Cirencester. His landlord, and indeed patron, was the 1st Earl Bathurst.

Toddington.

It was he, probably, who suggested to Rudder that Sir Robert Atkyns' history needed updating. So in 1779 *A New History of Gloucestershire* appeared, printed and published by Samuel.

Upper Slaughter.

Upper Slaughter

Perhaps the best known of Gloucestershire's diarists, thanks to publication of extracts, the **Rev. Francis Edward Witts** born at Cheltenham in 1783 served as rector here from 1808 till his death in 1854. His day-to-day account included not only parochial activities but also his duties as a magistrate, chairman of Stow Board of Guardians, trustee of Stow Provident bank, and many other committees. Interestingly the Witts family provided rectors here in unbroken succession from 1808 to 1913.

Weston-sub-Edge

William Latimer classical scholar and rector of Saintbury lived much of the time here, at Latimer's House.

Westonbirt

The Holford family had owned land in the south of the county since the sixteenth century, but it was **Robert Stayner Holford** who transformed Westonbirt. Money from his work as a lawyer and Master in Chancery, as well as investments in the New River Company allowed him to turn his attention to rebuilding a great mansion in 1863 and continue laying out the extensive arboretum. The latter's 600 acres and 3000 woody plants made it the largest in Europe. By the time of his death in 1892 it had attracted an international reputation. Incidentally the Holford's London house has been replaced in Park Lane by the Dorchester Hotel.

Winchcombe

John Smalwoode was born in this town and probably his would have been an uneventful life, but for the move he made to Berkshire where his apprenticeship to a draper led to a prosperity which merited the description, 'the most considerable clothier England ever beheld'. He not only became a pioneer of clothing manufacture, he also equipped and led 100 men in an expedition to counter Scotland's war, a campaign which ended disastrously at Flodden in 1513. Perhaps he is better known as Jack of Newbury; indeed his fame spread before that of the other Gloucestershire worthy Dick Whittington.

The chief cult personality here, though, was

'The Corner Cupboard', Winchcombe.

St Kenelm who reputedly was murdered at the age of seven by his sister having succeeded to the crown of his father King Kenulf. A shrine at the abbey attracted pilgrims from the ninth century till the Dissolution of the Monasteries in the sixteenth century.

Not quite so unfortunate as Kenelm but nevertheless a victim of events, **Christopher Merrett** saw his life's work go in flames. He was born at Winchcombe in 1614, his family home being the present 'Corner Cupboard'. After Oxford University he became Librarian and Fellow of the Royal College of Physicians. In 1666 his great book *Pinax Rerum* was published, describing over 1400 species of animals, plants and fossils, and containing the first listing of British birds. Sadly that year also saw the Great Fire of London, and poor Merrett had to witness not only the destruction of his book, but also the library and with it the loss of his job.

The ruined tower at Sudeley castle, Winchcombe, where George III tumbled down the stairs.

After Henry VIII died in 1547 his widow **Katherine Parr** married Thomas Seymour, and the following year they came to live here at nearby Sudeley castle. It was not a happy time for in September she died after giving birth to a daughter. Lady Jane Grey was chief mourner at the funeral, but she was not the only Queen to stay at Sudeley: Anne Boleyn and Elizabeth I came too. And kings Richard III, Charles I, and George III were also here, though in greatly differing circumstances.

Woodchester

Perhaps the most romantic 'ruin' in Gloucestershire, Woodchester Park, an unfinished mansion set in a wooded valley, was the fantasy of **William Leigh**. A wealthy Roman Catholic, he conceived the idea of building a palace which would offer hospitality to the Pope in the event of Napoleon III occupying the Vatican States in the 1860s. To this end no expense was to be too great. The renowned architect of Gothic style, A. W. Pugin, was engaged, but Leigh decided his design was going to prove too costly. So another architect took his place, the local Benjamin Bucknall from Rodborough. For over a decade work progressed, but then Leigh died and his son abandoned the project.

At South Woodchester, **A. E. Housman** frequently visited Woodchester

Isaac Pitmans' house in Wotton-under-Edge.

House where his mother and cousins had close associations, indeed the poet and Latin scholar made it his second home.

Wotton-under-Edge

It was not until he was twenty-three that the Wiltshire-born **Isaac Pitman** came in 1836 to this town as a master of the newly-established British school. Because of his conversion to the Swedenborgian sect his appointment lasted less than a year. However, he then opened his own private school which gave him the opportunity of teaching the boys, many of whom had followed his change of location, his shorthand system. By the time he moved on in 1839 to Bath, Pitman's shorthand had been well tested, and the next fifty years saw recognition worldwide for the phonography, as well as a knighthood for the inventor.

Isaac Pitman

Like Pitman, **John Biddle** was a dissenter from the established church. Born in Wotton in 1615 the son of a tailor, he went to Oxford University, thanks to the help of his patron Lord Berkeley. After graduating he became master of St Mary de Crypt school in Gloucester, but his writing of a tract arguing for Unitarianism result in imprisonment till 1658. But his resolution and independence of belief bought more imprisonment from which he died in 1662.

Rowland Hill on the other hand had a more rewarding life as a preacher. The sixth son of Sir Rowland Hill, he was born at Hawkstone Park, Shropshire in 1744 and ordained in 1773. His evangelistic powers developed whilst a curate in Somerset; such was his following that a chapel was built for him at Wotton. Every year of his life he would return to preach here. He championed Jenner's campaign for vaccination, and was a leader in the Religious Tract Society and the London Missionary Society, as well as opening the first London Sunday school.

Wyck Rissington

At the age of seventeen years **Gustav Holst** secured his first appointment as organist to this place, at an annual salary of £4. From May 1892 he spent the weekend here travelling by train from Cheltenham to Bourton-on-the-Water, and walking from there. He lodged with a choirman's family at a house on the green, returning to Cheltenham each Monday. This arrangement lasted for twelve months, till he went to study at the Royal College of Music, in London.

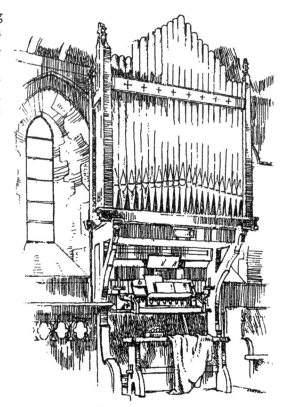

The organ at Wyk Rissington Church.

Index

Abbey, Edwin (artist). *Fairford*
Abercrombie, Lascelles (poet). *Dymock*
Anne, Princess. *Minchinhampton*
Archer, Fred (jockey). *Cheltenham, Prestbury*
Archer-Shee, George (naval cadet). *Nailsworth*
Ashbee, C. R. (architect). *Chipping Campden*
Atkyns, Robert (antiquary). *Duntisbourne Rouse, Sapperton*
Awdry, W. Awdry (writer). *Stroud*

Bacon, Francis (artist). *Prescott*
Bacon, Roger (scientist). *Bussage*
Baker, Barwick (landowner, philanthropist). *Hardwicke*
Barnett, John (composer). *Cheltenham*
Barnsley, Ernest and Sidney (craftsmen). *Duntisbourne Rouse, Sapperton*
Bayly, Thomas Haynes (poet). *Cheltenham*
Beale, Dorothea (educationist). *Cheltenham*
Beerbohm, Max (writer). *Edge, Oakridge*
Bennett, Eugene VC. *Stroud*
Berkeley family (landowners). *Berkeley*
Biddle, John (educationist). *Wotton-under-Edge*
Boevey, Catharine (benefactress). *Flaxley*
Boughton, Rutland (composer). *Kilcot*
Boyes, Duncan VC. *Cheltenham*
Bradley, A. C. (writer). *Cheltenham*
Bradley, James (astronomer). *Minchinhampton, Sherborne*
Bronowski, Jacob (scientist, writer). *Cleeve Hill*
Brooke, Charles (administrator). *Cirencester*
Brooke, Rupert (poet). *Dymock*
Browne, Dr (physician). *Minchinhampton*
Buchanan, Angus VC. *Coleford*
Bucknall, Benjamin (architect). *Rodborough*
Budding, Edward (inventor). *Thrupp*
Burton, Clara (artist). *Charlton Kings*
Butler, John Fitzhardinge VC. *Berkeley*

Butler, Josephine (reformer). *Cheltenham*
Butler, R. A. (politician). *Minchinhampton*

Canton, John (inventor). *Stroud*
Carroll, Lewis (writer). *Charlton Kings*
Cartland, Barbara (writer). *Tewkesbury*
Chadwick, Lynn (sculptor). *Bisley*
Charles I. *Matson, Painswick*
Charles, Prince of Wales. *Tetbury*
Clark, Leonard (poet). *Cinderford*
Clifford, Jane. *Frampton-on-Severn*
Close, Francis (cleric). *Cheltenham*
Cockerell, Charles (landowner). *Sezincote*
Colledge, Thomas (physician). *Cheltenham*
Courtauld, Samuel (merchant). *Minchinhampton*
Coxe, Charles (judge). *Bisley*
Craik, Mrs (writer). *Amberley, Charlton Kings, Tewkesbury*
Craven, Fulwar (eccentric). *Brockhampton*

Daukes, Samuel (architect). *Cheltenham*
Davies, W. H. (writer). *Nailsworth*
Day-Lewis, Cecil (writer). *Charlton Kings*
Deane, Richard (soldier). *Temple Guiting*
Delius, Frederick (composer). *Stroud*
Dobell, Sydney (poet). *Amberley, Charlton Kings*
Dover, Robert (promoter). *Aston-sub-Edge, Chipping Campden*
Dowty, George (engineer). *Cheltenham*
Drinkwater, John (writer). *Dymock, Oakridge*
Dunraven, Countess of. *Clearwell*

Edwards, David (cleric). *Stinchcombe*
Eliot, T. S. (poet). *Ashton-sub-Edge*
Elliott, John (cleric). *Randwick*
Enoch, Richard (collector). *Stow-on-the-Wold*

Farjeon, Eleanor (writer). *Dymock*
Finzi, Gerald (composer). *Painswick*
Flecker, James Elroy (poet). *Cheltenham, Cranham*
Forbes, John (architect). *Cheltenham*
Forbes-Robertson, James VC. *Cheltenham*
Fox, Edward (cleric). *Dursley*

Frost, Robert (poet). *Dymock*

Gere, Charles (artist). *Amberley, Gloucester, Painswick*
Gibbs, J. Arthur (writer). *Ablington*
Gibson, Wilfred (poet). *Dymock*
Gimson, Ernest (craftsman). *Duntisbourne Rouse, Sapperton*
Goldsmid, Francis (landowner). *Rendcomb*
Gordon, Adam Lindsay (poet). *Cheltenham*
Greene, Graham (writer). *Chipping Campden*
Griggs, F. L. (artist). *Chipping Campden*
Grisewood, Frederick (broadcaster). *Daylesford*
Grove, C. (cleric). *Tewkesbury*
Guise, Christopher, Berkeley, John Wright and William (landowners). *Elmore*
Guise, John VC. *Highnam*
Gurney, Ivor (musician, poet). *Gloucester*
Gwinnett, Button (administrator). *Down Hatherley*

Hale, Matthew (lawyer). *Alderley*
Hall, Marie (musician). *Cheltenham*
Hanbury-Tracy, Charles (landowner). *Toddington*
Handley Page, Frederick (engineer). *Cheltenham*
Hanger, George (landowner). *Kempsford*
Harmsworth, E. Cecil (newspaper magnate). *Daylesford*
Harris, Sir Arthur (airman). *Cheltenham*
Harrison, William (steward). *Chipping Campden*
Hart, Richard (monk). *Brockworth*
Hartley, B. (journalist). *Prescott*
Harvey, Frederick (poet). *Minsterworth*
Hastins, Warren (administrator). *Daylesford*
Hayward, Dr (physician). *Minchinhampton*
Henley, W.E. (poet). *Gloucester*
Hicks-Beach, Michael (politician). *Coln St Aldwyns*
Hill, Rowland (evangelist). *Wotton-under-Edge*
Hodgson, Brian (botanist). *Alderley*
Holford, Robert (landowner). *Westonbirt*
Hollis, George VC. *Chipping Sodbury*
Holmes, William VC. *Stanway*
Holst, Gustav (composer). *Cheltenham, Cranham, Wyck Rissington*
Hook, Alfred VC. *Churcham*
Hooper, John (cleric). *Gloucester*
Hopkins, John (hymnographer). *Awre*

Horlick, James (inventor). *Cowley*
Housman, A.E. (writer). *Woodchester*
Howells, Herbert (composer). *Lydney*
Howitt, Mary (writer). *Coleford*
Howse, Joseph (explorer). *Cirencester*
Hulls, Jonathan (inventor). *Chipping Campden*
Hulton, Edward (publisher). *Salperton*
Hyde-White, Wilfred (actor). *Bourton-on-the-Water*

Ind, Alfred VC. *Tetbury*

Jearrad, C. and R. W. (architects). *Cheltenham*
Jelf family (boatmen). *Ashleworth*
Jenner, Edward (physician). *Berkeley, Kingscote*
Jessop, Gilbert (cricketer). *Cheltenham*
Johnson, Amy (aviator). *Stoke Orchard*
Johnson, Dudley VC. *Bourton-on-the-Water*
Jones, Samuel (cleric). *Tewkesbury*

Kean, Edmund (actor). *Stroud*
Keble, John (cleric). *Coln St Aldwyns, Fairford, Southrop*
Keble, Thomas (cleric). *Bisley*
Keck, Anthony (architect). *Kings Stanley*
Kenelm (saint and martyr). *Winchcombe*
Kent, Prince and Princess Michael. *Bisley*
Keyte, William (landowner). *Ashton-Sub-Edge*
Kilby, Arthur VC. *Cheltenham*
Kingston, William (landowner). *Flaxley*
Kitcat, Sidney (cricketer). *Tetbury*
Knipe, Joseph (educationist). *Cirencester*
Kyrle, John (philanthropist). *Dymock*

Latimer, William (cleric). *Saintbury, Weston-Sub-Edge*
Lee, Laurie (writer). *Slad*
Leigh, Thomas (cleric). *Adlestrop*
Leigh, William (landowner). *Woodchester*
Liddell, Alice. *Tetbury*
Lister, R. Ashton (engineer). *Dursley*
Lysons family (antiquaries). *Rodmarton*
Lysons, Henry VC. *Rodmarton*

McCarthy, Lillah (actress). *Cheltenham*
McDonell, William VC. *Cheltenham*
Macmillan, Maurice (politician). *Tetbury*
Macready, Charles (actor). *Cheltenham*
Mansbridge, Albert (educationist). *Gloucester*
Marling, Percival VC. *King's Stanley*
Masefield, John (writer). *Duntisbourne Rouse, Pauntley*
Maskelyne, John (illusionist). *Cheltenham*
Mason, Charles (surveyor). *Sapperton*
Massingham, H. J. (writer). *Chipping Campden*
Merrett, Christopher (writer). *Winchcombe*
Middleton, John (architect). *Cheltenham*
Midwinter, William (cricketer). *St Briavels*
Miles, Frances VC. *Clearwell*
Moore, John (writer). *Tewkesbury*
Mulock, Dinah *see* Craik, Mrs
Mushett, Robert (ironmaster). *Coleford*

Napier, Charles (soldier). *Cheltenham*
North, Marianne (artist). *Alderley*

Orwell, George (writer). *Cranham*

Papworth, John (architect). *Cheltenham*
Parr, Queen Katherine. *Winchcombe*
Parry, Caleb (physician). *Cirencester*
Parry, Hubert (composer). *Highnam*
Parry, Thomas Gambier (artist). *Highnam*
Parry, William (explorer). *Cirencester*
Pate, Richard (philanthropist). *Cheltenham*
Paul, Geroge Onesiphorus (reformer). *Rodborough*
Pearce, Simon (entrepreneur). *Randwick*
Pedersen, Mikael (inventor). *Dursley*
Pitman, Isaac (inventor). *Wotton-under-Edge*
Pope, Alexander (writer). *Cirencester*
Porter, Endymion (poet). *Aston-Sub-Edge*
Potter, Dennis (writer). *Berry Hill*
Potter, Richard (magnate). *Standish*
Powle, Henry (politician). *Coln St Aldwyns*

Raikes, Robert (reformer). *Gloucester*

Ricardo, David (economist). *Minchinhampton*
Richardson, Ralph (actor). *Cheltenham*
Riviere, Briton (artist). *Charlton Kings*
Robins, Thomas (artist). *Charlton Kings*
Robinson, W. Heath (artist). *Cranham*
Rothenstein, William (artist). *Oakridge*
Rudder, Samuel (antiquary). *Rendcombe, Uley*
Rushout, James (landowner). *Blockley*

Sankey, John (politician). *Moreton-in-Marsh*
Shelley, Percy (poet). *Lechlade*
Smalwoode, John (clothier). *Winchcombe*
Smirke, Robert (architect). *Cheltenham*
Smith, C. Aubrey (actor). *Chipping Campden*
Smith, John Stafford (composer). *Gloucester*
Smythe, Pat (horsewoman). *Miserden*
Southcott, Joanna (prophetess). *Blockley*
Spencer, Stanley (artist). *Leonard Stanley*
Spencer-Churchill family. *Blockley*
Steer, P. Wilson (artist). *Gloucester*
Sternhold, Thomas (hymnographer). *Blakeney*
Stevens, George (jockey). *Cleeve Hill*
Sturt, Charles (explorer). *Cheltenham*
Sumsion, Herbert (composer). *Gloucester*

Tame, John (merchant). *Fairford*
Taylor, John (poet). *Gloucester*
Tennyson, Alfred Lord (poet). *Cheltenham*
Theyer, John (antiquary). *Blockworth*
Thomas, Edward (poet). *Dymock*
Throckmorton, John (landowner). *Bisley*
Tracy, William. *Toddington*
Tyndale, William (scholar). *Slimbridge*

Wade, Charles (collector). *Snowshill*
Wager, Charles (sailor). *Charlton Kings*
Warlock, Peter (composer). *Didbrook*
Warner family. *Blockley*
Warren, C. Henry (writer). *Edge*
Watkins, Miles (eccentric). *Cheltenham*
Waugh, Evelyn (writer). *Stinchcombe*

Wemyss, Earl and Countess (landowners). *Stanway*
Wesley, Samuel Sebastian (composer). *Gloucester*
West, Richard VC. *Cheltenham*
Wheatstone, Charles (inventor). *Gloucester*
Whitefield, George (evangelist). *Gloucester*
Whittington, Richard (merchant). *Coberley, Pauntley*
Williams, Isaac (cleric). *Stinchcombe*
Williams, Ralph Vaughan(composer). *Down Ampney*
Wilson, Edward (explorer). *Cheltenham*
Wilson, Ernest (botanist). *Chipping Campden*
Witts, Francis (diarist). *Upper Slaughter*
Wood, Mrs Henry (writer). *Newnham-on-Severn*
Wood, James (merchant). *Gloucester*
Woodhouse, Violet (musician). *Bisley*
Wren, P.C. (writer). *Amberley*

Yorke, Henry (writer). *Forthampton*
Yorke, Philip and Charles (lawyers). *Hardwicke*
Young, Jimmy (broadcaster). *Cinderford*